CREATING COMICS

CREATING MANGA COMICS

NEW YORK

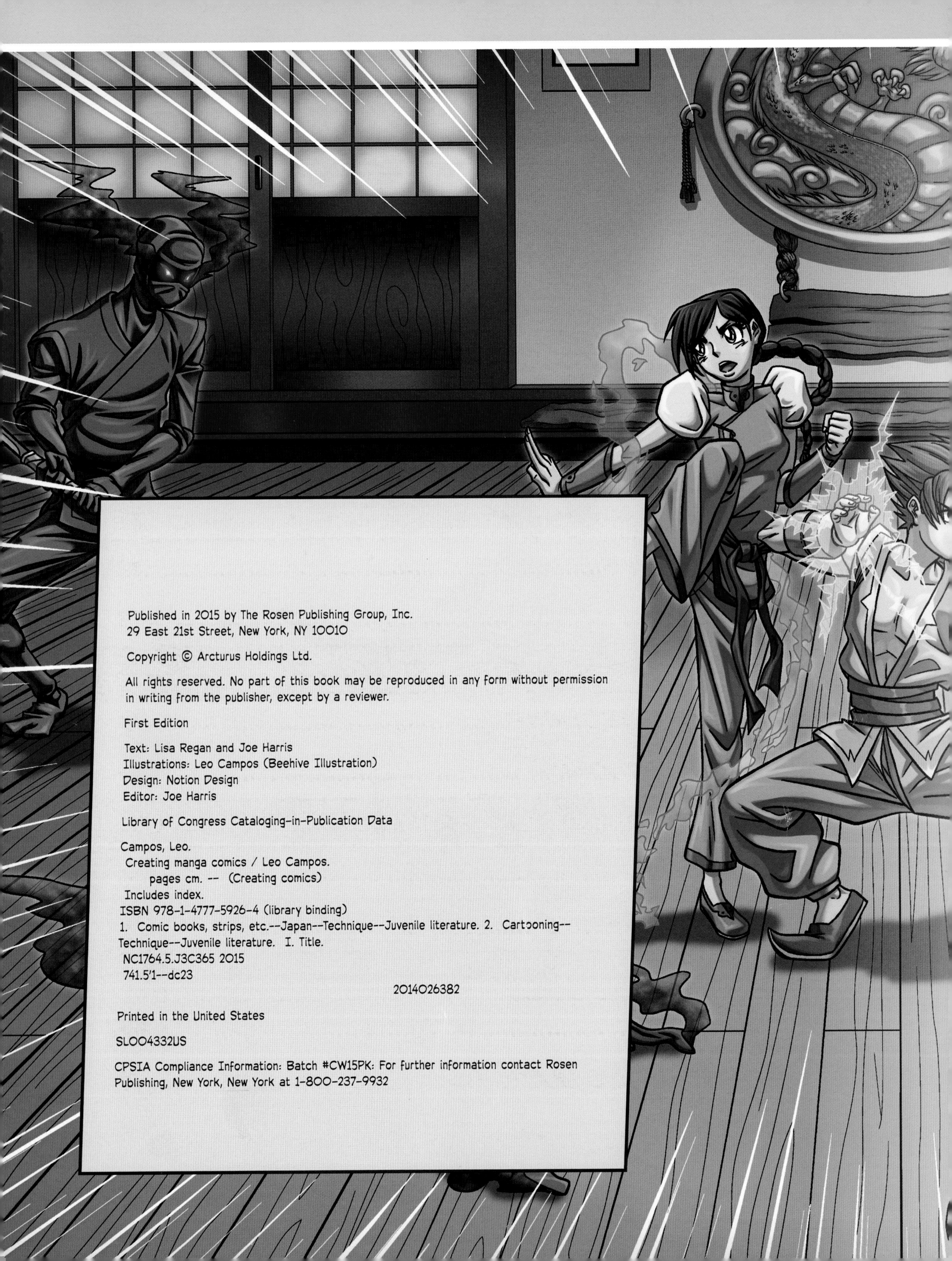

Published in 2015 by The Rosen Publishing Group, Inc.
29 East 21st Street, New York, NY 10010

First Edition

Text: Lisa Regan and Joe Harris
Illustrations: Leo Campos (Beehive Illustration)
Design: Notion Design
Editor: Joe Harris

Library of Congress Cataloging-in-Publication Data

Campos, Leo.
Creating manga comics / Leo Campos.
pages cm. -- (Creating comics)
Includes index.
ISBN 978-1-4777-5926-4 (library binding)
1. Comic books, strips, etc.--Japan--Technique--Juvenile literature. 2. Cartooning--Technique--Juvenile literature. I. Title.
NC1764.5.J3C365 2015
741.5'1--dc23
2014026382

Printed in the United States

SL004332US

CPSIA Compliance Information: Batch #CW15PK: For further information contact Rosen Publishing, New York, New York at 1-800-237-9932

CONTENTS

TOOLS OF THE TRADE

THE GREAT THING ABOUT DRAWING MANGA IS THAT YOU DON'T NEED EXPENSIVE EQUIPMENT TO GET STARTED. JUST GRAB THE ITEMS BELOW, AND YOU'RE READY TO GO!

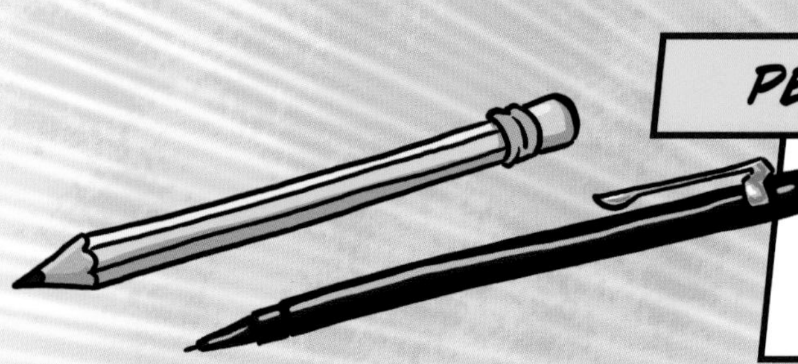

PENCILS

Soft (B, 2B) pencils are great for drawing loosely and are easy to erase. Fine point pencils are handy for adding detail.

ERASERS

A kneaded eraser molds to shape, so you can use it to remove pencil from tiny areas. Keep a clean, square-edged eraser to hand, too.

PENS

An artist's pens are his or her most precious tools! Gather a selection with different tips for varying the thickness of your line work.

FINE LINE AND BRUSH PENS

Fine line pens are excellent for small areas of detail. Brush pens are perfect for varying your line weight or shading large areas.

PENCILS, INKS, AND COLORS

HERE ARE THE FOUR MAIN STAGES OF CREATING A COLOR PICTURE. MANGA IS USUALLY PRINTED IN BLACK AND WHITE, BUT YOU CAN USE AS MUCH COLOR AS YOU LIKE!

ROUGH SKETCHES

Start by doing a rough sketch of your character. Use simple pencil lines and shapes. Work out their pose and proportions before adding details.

TIGHT SKETCHES

When you are happy with your sketch, it is time to draw over it with clean, firm pencil lines. Then erase your rough strokes, and add shading and detail.

INKS

Now it's time to finalize your line work by adding inks and erasing pencil lines. For a traditional black-and-white manga look, finish at this stage.

COLORS

By adding color to your image, you can really bring it to life. Traditional manga stories only use color on their covers, but you can make your own rules.

DRAWING HUMAN FIGURES

IT'S IMPORTANT TO THINK ABOUT PROPORTIONS WHEN DRAWING YOUR MANGA CHARACTERS. IF YOUR FIGURES' ARMS OR LEGS ARE THE WRONG LENGTH, THOSE BASIC ERRORS WILL STICK OUT LIKE A SORE THUMB!

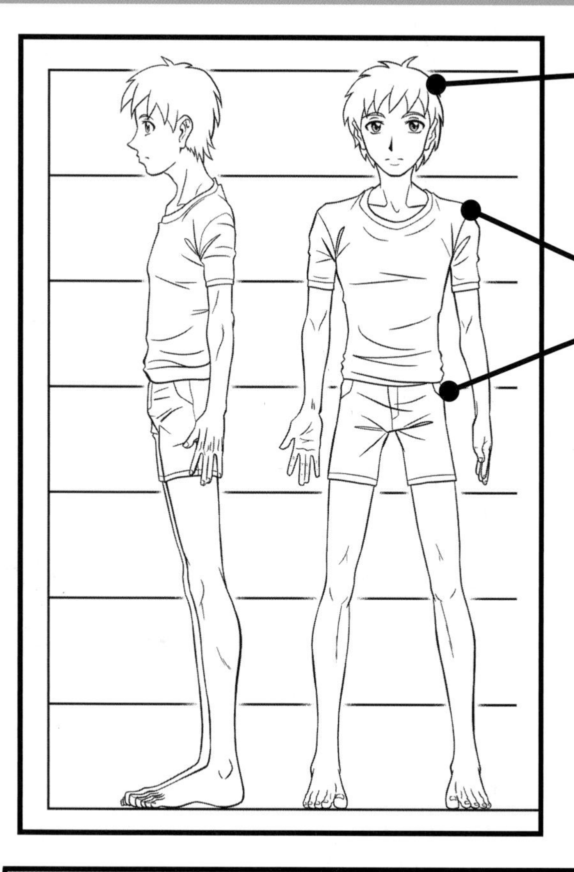

HEADS

Think of your characters' heights in terms of a number of "heads." A typical manga character is about seven heads tall.

SHOULDERS AND HIPS

Male characters are broadest at their shoulders. Female characters are broadest at their hips.

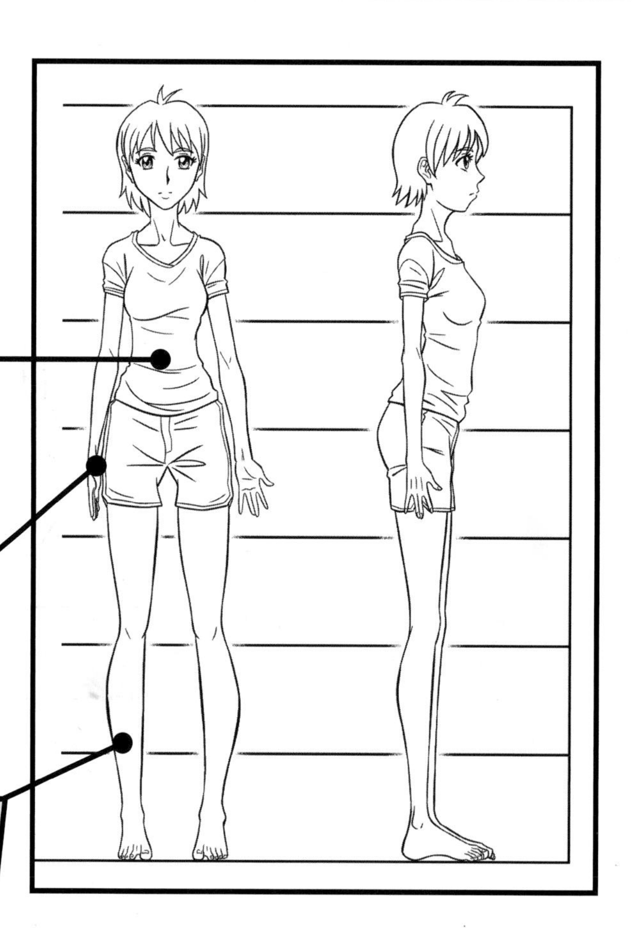

TORSOS

The average character's torso measures about two and a half head lengths.

ARMS

Arms reach from the shoulder down to the midpoint of the thigh. Be careful not to give your characters apelike arms!

LEGS

Manga characters' legs measure about four head lengths.

DRAWING HEADS

BY REMEMBERING A FEW SIMPLE RULES, YOU CAN MAKE SURE THAT YOUR FACES LOOK APPEALING. THIS WILL ALSO HELP WITH KEEPING FACES CONSISTENT FROM ONE PANEL TO THE NEXT.

FRONT VIEW

In manga, as in real life, eyes are positioned about halfway down the head. But manga eyes are much larger than real ones!

SIDE VIEW

Manga noses are almost invisible when shown head-on. From the side, they are cute and pointed, extending for roughly one eye-height.

BOYS AND GIRLS

Male and female characters both have slim faces. Girls' faces tend to be narrower, with a more pointed chin. They also have longer eyelashes.

EYEBROWS AND EARS

In manga, both male and female eyebrows are narrow and gently arched. Ears extend from the top of the eyes to the bottom of the nose.

HOW TO DRAW

A MONSTER TRAINER

IT'S TIME TO TACKLE YOUR FIRST MANGA CHARACTER! MEET OUR MAGICAL TRAINER, TOKIKO, AND HER TAME MONSTER. THE CREATURE IS A KITSUNE, A MYTHOLOGICAL FOX WITH SUPERNATURAL ABILITIES. KITSUNES HAVE MANY TAILS, WHICH SHOW THEIR AGE AND POWER.

1 All your sketches should start with a wireframe. This allows you to get the stance and proportions correct.

2 Roughly sketch in all the elements of the image, from the *kitsune*'s nine tails to the trainer's talismans. She is carrying a magical wand with streamers, called an *ounusa*.

3 When the proportions are correct, flesh out the figure with clothes and features. Add a high ponytail for dramatic effect and chunky boots to contrast with her frilled skirt. This girl means business!

4 Draw the final details of your image, including the flames at the *kitsune*'s feet. Pencil in folds on the clothes to give the picture movement and texture. Add an inscription on the trainer's *ofuda*—the cards held in her left hand.

5 Trace over the pencil lines of your image with ink. Then use an eraser to clean everything up. A well-inked image should look sharp and crisp. Now you can see the amount of work that goes into every panel of a manga story!

6 The addition of color is often the most fun part of the process. Manga characters express their personalities through their clothes and hair as well as their faces. Use darker shades of the same colors for shading the image.

MANGA EYES

EYES ARE THE MOST IMPORTANT FEATURES ON A MANGA FACE. THEY ARE USED TO SHOW EMOTIONS AND ALSO HELP TO MAKE CHARACTERS LOOK LIKABLE AND SYMPATHETIC.

HAPPY EYES

Wide eyes and high eyebrows show happiness. The eyes are very reflective, and the bottom lids curve upward.

SADNESS

Sad characters tend to have actual tears in their eyes. Lower the eyelids and drop the outer eyebrows.

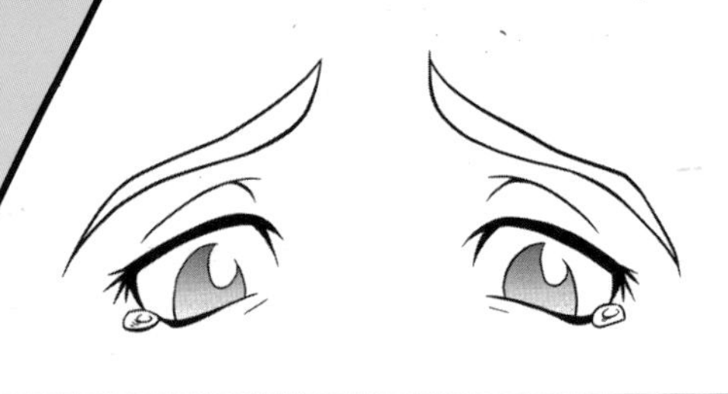

EMBARRASSMENT

The blush lines say "Cringe!" and a sideways glance adds to the impression that this character is feeling shame.

ANGER

The inner eyebrows are dramatically lowered to depict fury. The pupils are small and darker than usual.

FEAR/SHOCK

The contracted pupils have almost disappeared here, but the eyes themselves are large and wide with fear.

MANGA HAIR

HAIRSTYLES CAN SAY A LOT ABOUT A MANGA HERO OR HEROINE. GENERALLY SPEAKING, THE BIGGER THE HAIR, THE WILDER THE CHARACTER!

SPIKY HAIR

Have fun with thick, spiked hair. Frame the face first, and then let it flow backward with jagged tufts.

SMART HAIR

Some manga characters have more realistic hairstyles. If the hair is black, add some white highlights.

RIBBONS

In manga, even tough girls love ribbons! Ponytails are a great device for showing movement.

WINDBLOWN HAIR

It's very common in manga to show hair being blown about by the wind.

HOW TO DRAW

A MARTIAL ARTIST

MOST MANGA FANS LOVE A FIGHT SCENE! CAPTURING A MARTIAL ARTIST IN ACTION CAN BE TRICKY. HOWEVER, IF YOU PAY CAREFUL ATTENTION TO GETTING THE WIREFRAME RIGHT, EVERYTHING ELSE WILL FALL INTO PLACE. OUR FIGHTER, KAZUO, IS WIELDING ENERGY NUNCHAKUS.

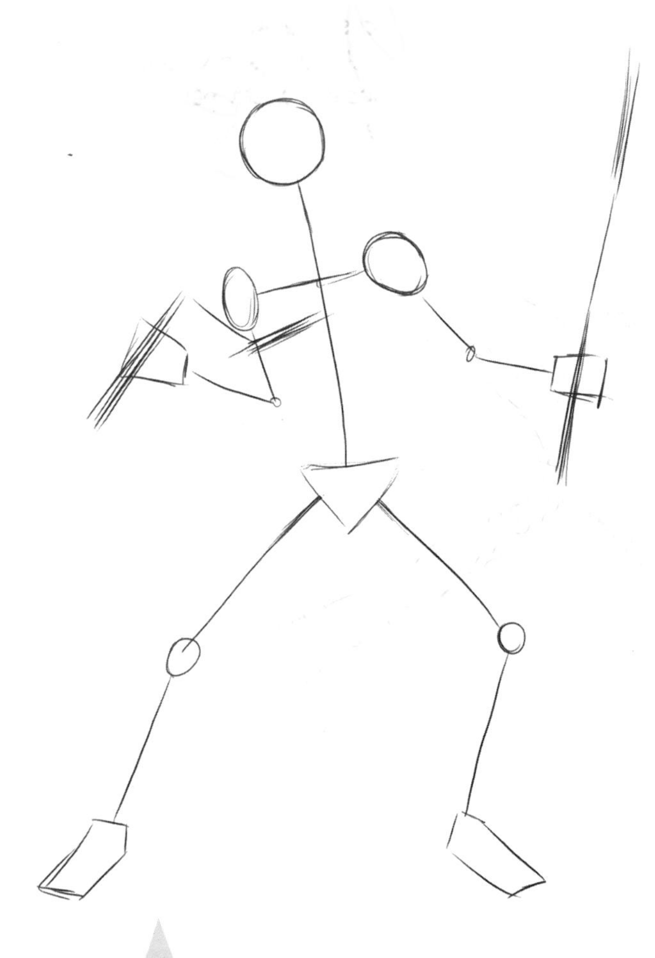

1 The fighting stance is well-balanced, with legs apart, arms wide, and feet planted securely but ready to spring.

2 Our fighter may be tough, but like most manga characters, he has a slim build. Take note of how the hands are drawn holding the weapons realistically.

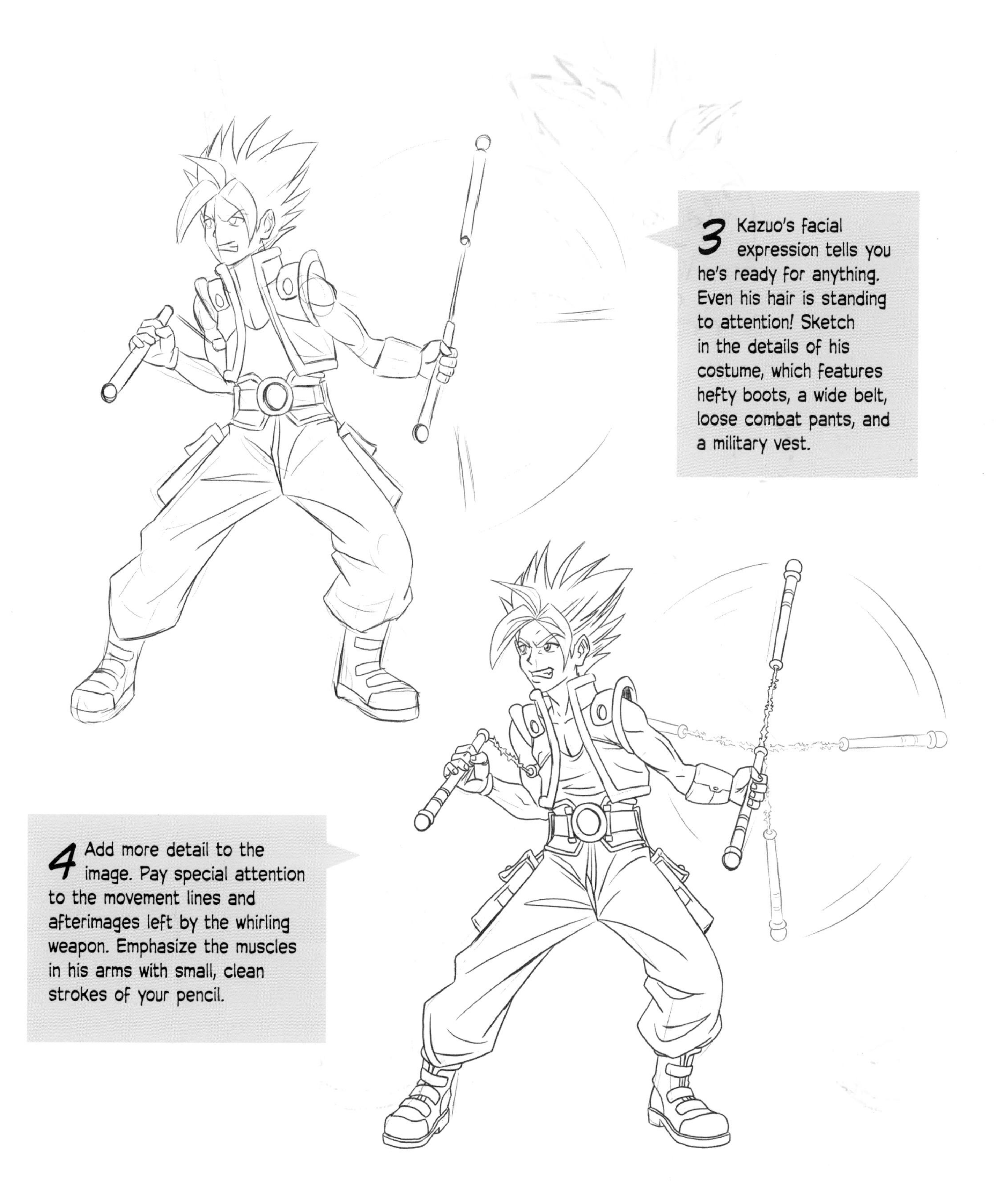

3 Kazuo's facial expression tells you he's ready for anything. Even his hair is standing to attention! Sketch in the details of his costume, which features hefty boots, a wide belt, loose combat pants, and a military vest.

4 Add more detail to the image. Pay special attention to the movement lines and afterimages left by the whirling weapon. Emphasize the muscles in his arms with small, clean strokes of your pencil.

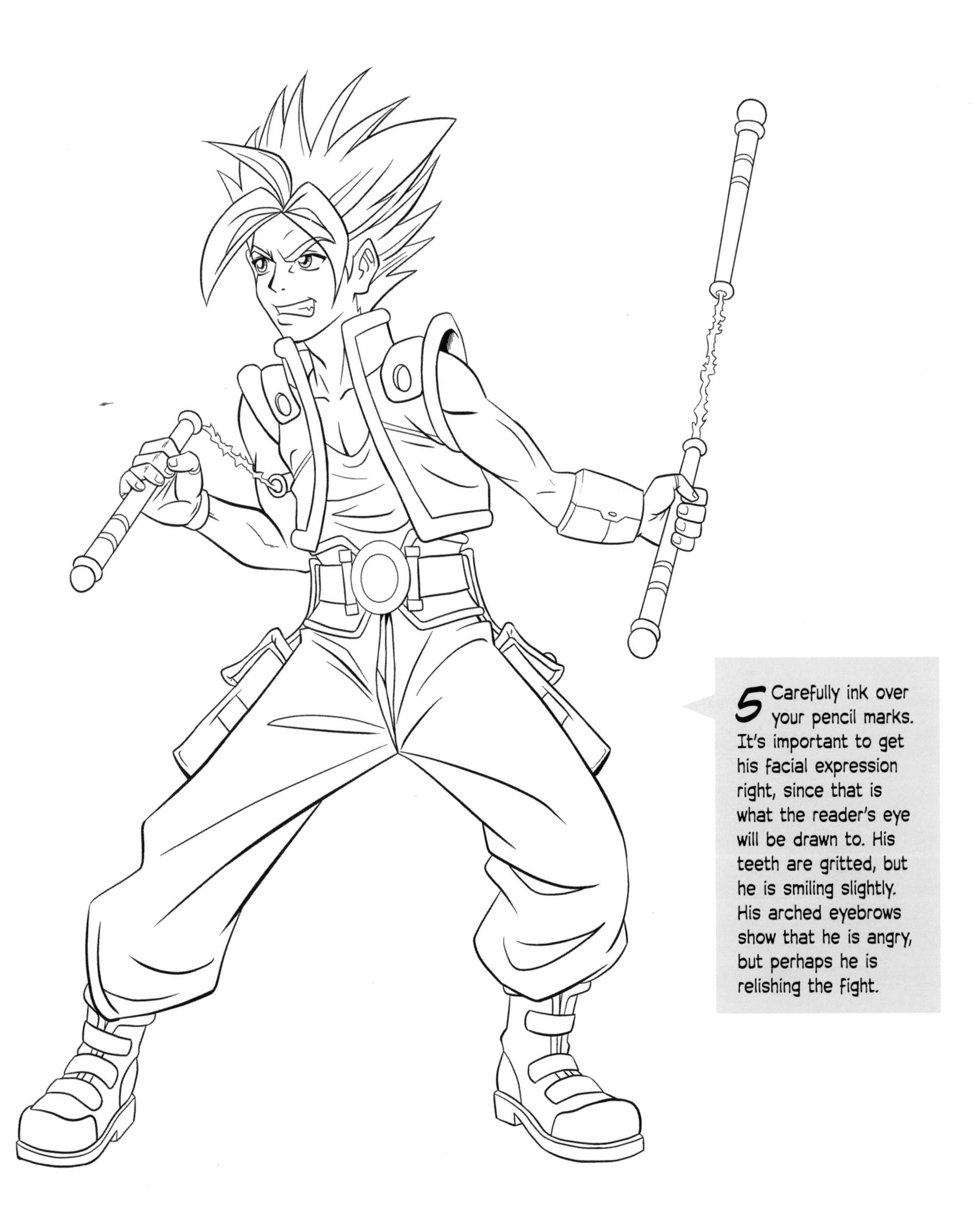

5 Carefully ink over your pencil marks. It's important to get his facial expression right, since that is what the reader's eye will be drawn to. His teeth are gritted, but he is smiling slightly. His arched eyebrows show that he is angry, but perhaps he is relishing the fight.

6 The basic blue color scheme here is calm, but the flashes of orange add flair and personality. No black is needed for the shading; the folds of his clothes use darker tones of the various blues. Silvery grays show the electric charge of his weapon.

SHOWING EMOTIONS

MANGA HAS ITS OWN WAYS OF SHOWING WHAT PEOPLE ARE FEELING. NOTE THAT THE EMOTIONS ARE CONVEYED BY BOTH THE CHARACTERS' EXPRESSIONS AND BY THE BACKGROUNDS.

CHIBI CARTOONS

IN MANGA, CHARACTERS' EMOTIONS ARE SOMETIMES SHOWN IN AN EXAGGERATED WAY BY DRAWING THE CHARACTERS AS CHIBIS FOR ONE OR MORE PANELS. CHIBIS ARE TINY AND CHILDLIKE, WITH A HEAD THAT'S ALMOST AS LONG AS THEIR BODY. THEY USUALLY HAVE NO NOSE!

HOW TO DRAW

THE DARK RONIN

TAKE A STEP INTO JAPANESE HISTORY WITH THIS TROUBLED WARRIOR. A RONIN IS A MASTERLESS SAMURAI, ARMED AND IN ARMOR, AND A MASTER OF MARTIAL ARTS AND COMBAT. ALL SAMURAI CARRY TWO SWORDS AND SOMETIMES OTHER WEAPONS, TOO.

1 Lightly sketch the wireframe, with a guarded stance and two lines for the *katanas*—long, curved Japanese swords.

2 Flesh out his broad chest and limbs—this is no skinny samurai! Make sure his hips are narrower than his shoulders. Pay close attention to the position of his legs and feet.

3 Add to his roguish qualities with long, loose bangs and a wayward ponytail. His samurai uniform covers his chest and thighs, with a sash belt tied at the waist. Both arms should be protected, but it looks like this isn't his first fight ...

4 A lot can be shown about a character by the way you draw his features and also his clothes. This warrior's bandaged wrist speaks volumes, as does his ripped sleeve. Go to town with the detailing on his leather armor.

5 Up close, you can see the glint in this ronin's eye—the one that isn't obscured by a scar, anyway. Have fun decorating his swords with ornate handle grips. Make sure the bulges of his muscles and the folds of his breeches are fluid and light.

6 When adding color to the warrior, remember that he is a dark soul with a rebellious streak. The clothing beneath his armor should be drab and plain, but he wears his samurai colors with pride. Keep the colors light on the sharp edges of his swords.

SPEED LINES

MANGA CHARACTERS ARE PART OF A STORYTELLING PROCESS WITH ITS OWN TRICKS AND TECHNIQUES. HERE'S HOW A MANGA ARTIST CARRIES THE READER ALONG WITH THE ACTION WHEN THINGS ARE MOVING FAST!

HORIZONTAL SPEED LINES

Neatly ruled parallel lines show the direction of movement. They can be spaced very tightly to show increased speed but tend to be spaced farther apart around elements like the face.

RADIAL SPEED LINES

A starburst of lines spreading from a central point can show rapid movement toward or away from the reader. The blank space where the lines would meet is the far distance.

SPECIAL EFFECTS

PATTERNED MANGA BACKGROUNDS DO THREE THINGS: THEY GRAB THE READER'S ATTENTION, THEY SHOW CHARACTERS' REACTIONS WITHOUT WORDS, AND THEY MAKE FOR AN INTERESTING BREAK FROM STANDARD BACKGROUND SCENERY.

SURPRISE!

What's happening here? The startling background grabs your attention and makes you want to know more. It's something amazing, judging by the lightning flashes!

FOCUS LINES

An explosion of lines drawn outward from a focal point makes you instantly aware of what's important in a scene. This can add to the feeling of drama and excitement.

HOW TO DRAW

A DOJO SCENE

YOU'VE PRACTICED DRAWING CHARACTERS WITH VARIED EXPRESSIONS AND MOVEMENTS, AND ADDING DRAMATIC EFFECTS. NOW IT'S TIME TO PUT ALL THOSE SKILLS TOGETHER TO CREATE AN ACTION-PACKED SCENE IN WHICH SEVERAL CHARACTERS INTERACT WITH EACH OTHER.

1 Take some time to sketch the position of each character. They should feel like they are interacting in a dramatic way. Where are they each looking? What are they about to do?

2 When you're happy with how the characters fill the frame, sketch the basic lines of the background. Flesh out each of the characters, making sure they are all in proportion to each other.

3 Slowly build up the details of the characters and scenery. Don't ruin your hard work by rushing! Ask yourself: Do any areas of the image need more interest? We added some empty robes at the bottom left, to suggest that the ninjas can turn to smoke.

4 As you ink the image, make sure that it's clear what's happening. Who are the good guys and who are the bad guys? Your scene is telling a story, so it's up to you to show what's taking place. Never lose sight of the big picture!

FEARLESS FACES

Remember what you have learned about manga features. Give your heroes big eyes and expressions of brave determination to contrast them with the masked baddies.

5 Finally, use your coloring to highlight the main characters and make the villains look sinister. Use bold shades in the center, and play with the special effects, adding flames, sparks, and force fields.

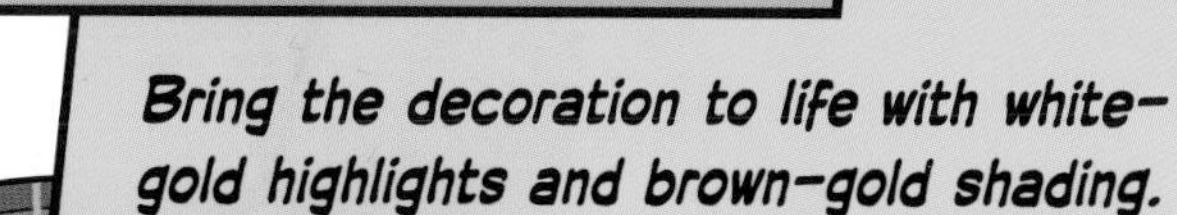

GOING FOR GOLD

Bring the decoration to life with white-gold highlights and brown-gold shading.

GLOWING EYES

Leave the middle of the ninjas' eyes bright white, but color the area around them red.

GLOSSARY

CHIBI (CHEE-bee)
A small, cute character that shows extreme personality traits. Chibi means "little one" in Japanese.

DOJO (DOH-joh)
A room for training or a gathering place for students.

HIGHLIGHTS (HY-lytz)
The brighter parts of an image that show where light is shining on an object.

INTERACT (IN-turh-akt)
To act in a way that affects someone or something else.

KITSUNE (KEET-soo-nay)
A fox spirit from Japanese mythology. According to tradition, kitsune are able to cast spells and take on human appearance.

NINJA (NIN-jah)
A Japanese warrior skilled in stealth.

PROPORTIONS (proh-POUHR-shuhnz)
The size of body parts in relation to each other.

RELISH (REH-lish)
To take great pleasure in.

RONIN (ROH-nin)
A samurai who no longer has a master; a shameful status.

SAMURAI (SAM-muh-ry)
A noble warrior from Japanese history.

TALISMANS (TAL-ihz-manz)
Objects with magical power.

WIREFRAME (WYR-fraym)
The basic outline sketch of a character, showing posture and proportion.

FURTHER INFORMATION

WEBSITES

Due to the changing nature of internet links, PowerKids Press has developed an online list of Web sites related to the subject of this book. This site is updated regularly. Please use this link to access the list:

www.powerkidslinks.com/cc/manga

FURTHER READING

Crilley, Mark. *Mastering Manga with Mark Crilley: 30 Drawing Lessons from the Creator of Akiko.* Blue Ash, OH: Impact Books, 2012.

Hart, Christopher. *Young Artists Draw Manga.* New York: Watson-Guptill Publications, 2011.

Hart, Christopher. *Xtreme Art: Draw Manga Chibi!.* New York: Watson-Guptill Publications, 2004.

McCloud, Scott. *Making Comics: Storytelling Secrets of Comics, Manga, and Graphic Novels.* New York: William Morrow Paperbacks, 2006.

Southgate, Anna and Sparrow, Keith. *Manga Magic: Drawing Manga Expressions and Poses.* New York: Rosen Central, 2011.

Various Authors. *Manga Shakespeare.* New York: Harry N. Abrams, 2008.

INDEX